Contents

Dedication

To Videl, Vishal, and Valen: The heartbeats that give rhythm to my life, and the legacy brighter than any star

Harness Your Superpower By
Learning to Enjoy Being Alone

THE ART
OF BEING
ALONE

Inspired By
Jordan Peterson
How To Be Happy Alone

DAVE DRAYTON

This book is published by Therapy Seminary Publishers.

Paperback Edition: **ISBN: 978-1-963674-01-9**

First Edition: 2024

Forward

"You're Alone. So What?"

Look, I get it. Everywhere you turn, you're bombarded with stories of love, friendship, and how "togetherness" is the spice of life. And here you are, holding a book about the opposite: Being alone. It's not sexy, it's not trendy, but damn, is it necessary.

"The Art of Being Alone" isn't a guide on how to wallow in self-pity or a masterclass in hermit-ism. It's a brutally honest take on why solitude isn't the enemy, but the very thing that can set you free. Loneliness? It's a state of mind, not a sentence.

If you're expecting sugar-coated advice and hand-holding, put the book down. But if you're ready to confront the raw truth—that learning to be alone can be the most badass thing you ever do—then buckle up. Because this journey will strip away the societal BS and challenge every notion you have about "loneliness."

By the end, you won't just be okay with being alone. You'll freaking celebrate it.

Dive in if you dare. But remember: Alone doesn't mean lonely. It's high time you learned the difference.

Introduction

"The best thinking has been done in solitude."

- Thomas A. Edison

Have you ever found yourself sitting alone, engulfed in the quietness of your surroundings, with only the soft whisper of the wind and the echo of your thoughts as your company? Solitude is a concept that has intrigued and intimidated us throughout the ages. It is more than just the absence of company; it's a state of being, an experience where one can be alone with their thoughts, disconnected from the chaos of the outside world, a sanctuary of self-reflection and introspection.

In our bustling society, solitude often finds itself at odds with the constant chatter of the digital age. We're always connected, always in touch, forever plugged into a network of digital friends, influencers, and trending topics. The idea of disconnecting, of being alone with nothing but our thoughts for company, seems foreign, even frightening. The fear of being alone, this dread of solitude, is what some may call 'monophobia,' and it's more common than you might think.

But what if we've been looking at this all wrong? What if solitude isn't something to fear, but something to embrace? What if being alone could be a source of strength, a catalyst for personal growth, a wellspring of creativity, and a path to inner peace?

This book, 'The Art of Being Alone,' is your journey of exploration into the paradox of solitude, inspired by the profound teachings of renowned philosopher and psychologist, Jordan Peterson.

Welcome to a transformative journey, where we explore the profound power of solitude—an art that, once mastered, can unlock your superhuman potential and lead you to a life of unparalleled fulfillment.

Prepare to embark on a voyage that challenges the very fabric of our existence, one that is both an homage to the wisdom of ages past and a call to action for the modern soul.

The secrets of solitude have been whispered through the corridors of time by some of history's most influential thinkers, and their voices resonate with an enduring truth: solitude is not to be dreaded but celebrated. It is the crucible for self-transformation, the forge where greatness is born, and the gateway to a life of extraordinary contentment.

Our quest into the enigma of solitude draws inspiration from luminaries who dared to embrace their solitude and transform it into a wellspring of personal growth. We will traverse the intellectual landscapes of Friedrich Nietzsche, the audacious 19th-century German philosopher who saw solitude as the path to greatness. Nietzsche's radical ideas about morality, truth, and self-affirmation challenged the norms of his time, and his insight into the transformative power of solitude is nothing short of revelatory.

Nietzsche's message echoes through the ages, urging us to stand apart from the crowd, to face the solitude that often accompanies the journey to self-ownership. 'The individual has always had to struggle to keep from being overwhelmed by the tribe,' he reminds us. 'If you try it, you will be lonely often and sometimes frightened, but no price is too high to pay for the privilege of owning yourself.' Within his words lies a promise—a promise of profound transformation through solitude.

Yet, solitude is not merely the domain of philosophers; it transcends time and disciplines. From Henry David Thoreau's idyllic sojourn at Walden Pond to Søren Kierkegaard's relentless pursuit of individuality, from Rollo May's confrontation with existential isolation to Carl Jung's quest for individuation, each thinker offers a unique lens through which we can perceive and grasp the art of being alone.

Jordan Peterson, the modern luminary who has carved his niche in the annals of psychology and philosophy, illuminates the path to self-growth and resilience in solitude. His insights resonate with the timeless wisdom of those who walked this path before him, providing us with a contemporary guide to navigate the solitude of our era.

As we delve deeper into the heart of solitude, let us remember Nietzsche's words: 'Loneliness is one thing, solitude another.' Solitude is not a state of lacking but a state of abundance, a profound encounter with the self. In embracing solitude, we cultivate the strength, independence, and creativity that propel us toward the summit of our potential.

The promise of this journey is clear: solitude is the secret superpower you've been waiting to harness. It is the key that unlocks your most authentic self, the catalyst for your transformation, and the source of boundless contentment. As we embark on this odyssey, brace yourself for revelations that will forever alter your perception of solitude.

Are you ready to embrace your solitude? This book is your no-nonsense guide, your passport to unlocking your hidden potential. Join us as we navigate the intricacy of solitude, discovering the treasures that await within. Your adventure begins now.

Chapter 1

"Whenever you find yourself on the side of the majority, it's time to pause and reflect." -
Mark Twain

Look, we've all heard the spiel: loneliness is the modern-day equivalent of being chased by a saber-toothed tiger. A study from Harvard University showed that loneliness could be as lethal as downing a dozen tequila shots. But here's the thing: do you give a damn about what Harvard thinks? Probably not. You're more interested in wrestling with your own mind-goblins of solitude.

Loneliness, my friend, has turned into this big, ugly monster under our beds. Why the hell did alone-time, once considered sacred introspection, become a modern-day Voldemort? A name we dare not utter? Why do we treat solitude as if it's some digital-age leprosy?

I'm no guru, but I've danced with the same demons. My mind's playlist often had tracks like "Is there an off button to my weirdness?" or "Maybe if I reprogram my personality, friends will stick around."

After months of solitary confinement (I mean, introspection, accompanied by questionable music choices), I had a 'Eureka!' moment: I actually enjoy my own company. Always have. Like that time I would lock myself up and dive deep into the world of Tolkien, traveling to Middle-earth. Damn, those were good times.

Rummaging through the dusty corners of my memories, I asked, "Why did I chase the crowd when all I wanted was a close-knit circle?" I didn't want to be the guy who sips beer with folks today and bad-mouths them tomorrow. It wasn't about the number. It was the quest for societal validation.

Take, for instance, high school. There was this girl – an enigma amidst 150 chirping teenagers. While my newbie self managed to make friends, she remained a solitary figure. Despite being there longer than most, she was always the lone wolf. Eating alone, blending into the furniture, embarking on solo restroom adventures. Hell, even peeing in public is a group sport for girls, but she was the exception.

Asking around, the verdict was predictable: "She's different... you know, a bit off." Our fear of loneliness isn't a born trait. It's fed to us, one outsider story at a time. Every flick, every book hammers home the same message:

alone = loser.

Being labeled the 'weirdo'? That's a massive no-no in our playbook. The idea of being the odd one out, the misfit, is scarier than any ghost story.

Look, I get it. We're all puppeteered by society's judgments. We hesitate, overthink, doubt. Our dreams get buried under 'what will they think.' Heck, David Foster Wallace nailed it:

*"You'll stop worrying
what others think about
you when you realize
how seldom they do."*

But here's the kicker: what if our fear is just an illusion? A narrative we've been force-fed, only to realize it's not even our story. What if being alone isn't the enemy but our perceptions of it? I mean, let's get real here: the greatest ideas, the most profound thoughts, they all spark in solitude. It's where magic brews.

We're about to embark on a journey that may flip your worldview on its head. Dive into the depths of loneliness, not to drown, but to discover treasures. And believe me, the treasures I speak of are unlike anything you've known. The tales that follow are weird, wonderful, and, dare I say, a tad wild. The kind that makes you question everything you've ever believed about being alone.

Ready to unlock the secret chambers of solitude and redefine loneliness? There's so much more beneath the surface, waiting to be explored. The real question is, are you daring enough to dive deep? Because what you find might just blow your mind.

Okay, let's be brutally honest for a moment. The person who's most likely to give you crap in life? That's right - it's you. Before anyone even gets the chance to judge your mess of a life, you've already dished out your own critiques. Who the hell needs critics when you're your own harshest one?

I remember during my college days, I had this awkward five-month-long phase where friends? Forget about it. After a colossal fight with my crew, I was effectively a solo act. Everyone else was clumped in their neat little friend groups, giggling, sharing inside jokes, and there I was - the lone wolf. Of course, I masked my solitude with a veneer of indifference. And while I stayed busy, secretly orchestrating events, and pseudo-socializing, the brutal truth? I was alone. And man, did I have a great facade going on. People thought I was having the time of my life. Classic irony.

I felt like I was under some imaginary spotlight. Every giggle, every whisper, every look felt like a judgment. Even when no one gave a damn. This self-constructed pressure of "What if they think I'm a loner?" was always gnawing at me. And despite fleeting moments of confidence, I always found a way to pull myself back into self-pity.

Here's a punch in the gut: being alone? It doesn't make you pathetic. What's truly pathetic is believing you've been abandoned, left in the dust. Society has spoon-fed us this garbage idea that solitude equals loser status. News flash: it's utter BULLSHIT.

You gotta realize - you don't need an army of friends to plaster all over Instagram to prove you're worth a damn. The online world is just a mirage, man. It's all these perfectly framed snippets of life, which make you feel like you're the only outsider. But here's the kicker: solitude doesn't mean loneliness.

When I was scribbling down the words for this book, it was just me and my thoughts. No best buds. No partner in crime.

Some would argue, "Oh, he's in his 20s. Shouldn't he be out partying or chasing romance?" And sure, I could mope around in a blanket burrito binging Netflix. But I saw my solitude as an opportunity. An opportunity to sip coffee with mom, dive deep into my writing, and just freaking BE. Without society's endless chirping in my ear.

When you chuck out that heavy cloak of loneliness and embrace solitude, man, the world looks different. And trust me, it's a good kind of different. You're not waiting for the weekend or for someone's nod of approval. Every damn day is an adventure.

To quote Taylor Swift (yes, I'm going there),

"the scary thing is, you're on your own now. But the cool thing is, you're on your own now."

Chew on that.

Being alone? It's not a death sentence. It's a damn privilege. You're hanging with the coolest person: yourself. Before flipping further into this book, sit back. Ponder on this: Can you embrace solitude and turn it into an epic solo journey? If you can, well, let's rock and roll into this adventure. Let's dive into turning loneliness into badass solitude and then use that to level up in life. Ready, champ?

Part One: The No-Bullshit Guide to Being Authentic

Chapter 1.1 - Why Your Obsession with Loneliness Sucks

In our pop culture-obsessed world, we've all fantasized about our lives taking the narrative of a classic cinematic plot. And why not? The intoxicating blend of drama, plot twists, love stories – it's irresistible.

Think about it. The movies we love, the series we binge-watch, they all have some universal themes, right? The downtrodden protagonist, some insurmountable challenges, and the knight in shining armor or the best friend that rides in and saves the day. It's captivating, but let's not kid ourselves. We love those movies because they're not real, not the other way around.

My friend Greg had this bizarre ritual. Every time he faced any major decision, he'd ask himself, "What would James Bond do in this situation?" It was a joke, but also kind of not. Greg was caught up in this Hollywood narrative, believing that if he emulated Bond or any other cinematic hero, he'd magically transform his life. I remember once, he tried to scale a wall (yeah, a literal wall!) to impress someone at a party, thinking it was his 'Bond moment'. He ended up with a fractured arm and a bruised ego.

That's the dangerous game of molding your life around a romanticized version of a story. You start to believe that for life to be worthwhile, it has to be grandiose. And more importantly, that you need someone else to complete it. You're not waiting for Godot; you're waiting for the person from your favorite rom-com to waltz into your life and magically fix everything. But let's snap back to reality.

Do you remember that scene in 'The Matrix' when Neo is offered the red pill and the blue pill? The red pill represented an uncomfortable truth, while the blue pill was a comforting lie. Sometimes, the idea of romanticizing life feels like taking the blue pill. It's a cushioned, rose-tinted version of reality where you're constantly in the limelight. But, like Neo, maybe it's time to choose the red pill.

Face it: Your life is not a movie. There won't always be a climactic scene, a dramatic twist, or a fairytale ending. And that's okay. Life's beauty is in its unpredictability, its mundane moments, its quiet tragedies, and its small triumphs.

Instead of looking for someone to come along and "complete" your narrative, focus on being the hero of your own story. It's time to stop sidelining yourself, waiting for someone to rescue you from your own life. It's time to start valuing the person you see in the mirror every morning. It's time to live a life defined by your choices, not by a script you think you should be following. You are the writer, director, and lead actor in the grand movie of your life. How do you want your story to unfold?

Are you ready to take the red pill? Let's dive into the real world together. Because the only thing crueler than not living your life is waiting for someone else to come and live it for you.

Chapter 2 - The Cost of Living a Lie: Why Faking Sucks More Than You Think

"To thine own self be true, and it must follow, as the night the day, thou canst not then be false to any man." - William Shakespeare.

Being genuine has become one of life's great challenges, buried beneath layers of societal expectations, pop culture, and our insatiable thirst for validation. A quote from centuries ago hits hard today. Shakespeare might not have faced the pressure of Instagram filters, but he knew a thing or two about staying genuine in a world of facades.

There was a time I wore a mask. Not a literal one, but a façade constructed of pleasing nods, forced laughs, and pre-rehearsed replies. When people met me, they didn't see me; they encountered a carefully curated version of me.

Every summer, my friends and I went on a camping trip. We would sit around the fire, swapping stories. One time, John, a close friend, shared an anecdote from college days – a story I had been a part of. As he narrated, I realized I didn't remember half the details. I had been physically present but mentally occupied with thoughts of what I should say next, how to act, or what others were thinking about me. My constant yearning to be 'perfect' had robbed me of genuinely living the moment.

Our obsession with perfection is nothing more than an illusion. We're bombarded daily with images of impeccable lives, flawless bodies, and fairytale romances. We chase these images, not realizing they are as real as the mirage in a desert.

The irony is, in trying to fit a mold, we become forgettable. Authenticity, flaws and all, is what truly captivates. Ever met someone unapologetically themselves and felt an immediate connection or admiration? That's the power of authenticity.

Mia, a colleague from work, never seemed to fit the 'normal' parameters. She wore mismatched socks, spoke with an odd mix of accents, and danced even without music. Initially, many labeled her as 'weird.' But over time, people were drawn to her. Why? She was genuine. In a world of pretenses, Mia was a breath of fresh air.

However, peeling away those layers of inauthenticity isn't an overnight task. It's about acknowledging your quirks, understanding your feelings, and most importantly, respecting yourself enough to be honest about them.

Remember that moment in the movies when the main character takes off their glasses, lets down their hair, and suddenly they're transformed? Real life isn't that cinematic, but the sentiment holds. When you shed those expectations and just be, it's liberating.

There's no rulebook on being you. It's uncharted territory that only you can navigate. Be kind to yourself, learn and grow from missteps, and always cherish your uniqueness.

Let's take this journey together, embracing authenticity and understanding that every imperfection is a badge of your humanity. It's time to stare into that mirror and recognize, cherish, and celebrate the person staring back.

Chapter 3 – Being Unapologetically, Irrevocably You

"To be yourself in a world that is constantly trying to make you something else is the greatest accomplishment." – Ralph Waldo Emerson

---

Remember that time in high school when you dyed your hair neon green to fit in with the "cool kids" but ended up looking like a broccoli instead? Or that time you ditched your quirky shirt for a basic one because everyone else was doing it? Yeah, me too.

Why Fitting In Is Overrated

1. **The Tabbed Existence**: Picture your mind like a browser with an insane number of tabs open - one for each role you're trying to play. Before you know it, the original page, the real you, gets lost in the clutter.

2. **Chasing the Mirage**: We try to modify our personas for every Tom, Dick, and Harry. It's exhausting and guess what? No one really cares about the facade.

3. **The 'Self-Love' Irony**: After this roller-coaster of imitation, we resort to "self-love hacks" without even knowing our true selves. It's like putting on a Band-Aid without cleaning the wound.

Finding Yourself: The Actual Path to Self-Love

Having lurked around social media recently, I've noticed an absurd misrepresentation of "self-love." Suddenly, it's become synonymous with consumerism. Forget that. Here's a lowdown on the real shit:

Know Thyself: Dive deep. Beyond the social etiquettes and the filters. What ticks you? What triggers you?

According to Socrates - "An unexamined life is not worth living.".

In the maelstrom of life and amidst the constant noise of societal expectations, we often find ourselves adrift, unmoored from our true essence. Knowing oneself goes beyond the superficial labels we often attach to our personalities; it's about delving deep into the recesses of our souls to uncover the hidden gems of our true nature.

Beyond the many masks of social etiquettes, beyond the layers of politeness and the charade we often play to fit in, lies a unique individual with dreams, fears, hopes, and scars. But who are you when there's no audience, when the world's spotlight doesn't shine on you, when there's no one to impress or appease?

Reflect on what truly moves you. It's not just about the beliefs that have been handed down to you or the values that society champions. It's about what resonates with you on a personal level, how these beliefs and values have subtly sculpted your decisions, your perspectives, and ultimately, your life's trajectory.

Understanding your emotional landscape is like charting a previously unexplored territory. The highs, the lows, the calm plateaus, and the turbulent waters, all play a crucial role. Recognizing these emotions, understanding what gives birth to them, and managing them is the first step toward emotional maturity.

Yet, as you embark on this enlightening journey, you'd also become acutely aware of your triggers, those situations or behaviors that throw you off balance, challenge your peace, or even ignite storms within. Recognizing these triggers is akin to seeing the bends in a river from a distance, allowing you to navigate through life's challenging terrains with increased dexterity and grace.

1. **Embrace Thyself**: The good, the bad, the downright ugly. Locking away your shadows doesn't help; it just amplifies them.

According to Brené Brown –

_____

"Owning our story and loving ourselves through that process is the bravest thing that we'll ever do."

_____

Embracing oneself isn't just a profound act of self-love; it's a revolutionary act in a world that often demands conformity. It's not just about the good days, the achievements, the moments that make you swell with pride. It's about the entire spectrum of your experiences, your life in all its hues.

Celebrate your strengths and achievements, for they are the pillars that hold you up, the winds beneath your wings. But equally, if not more importantly, acknowledge your flaws, your mistakes, your regrets. Instead of being chains that bind you, let them be the lessons that guide you. They are a testament to your journey, a journey that is uniquely yours.

The deepest fears, insecurities, and traumas often remain buried, casting long, ominous shadows over our lives. While confronting them can be a Herculean task, it's a step forward toward healing, toward liberation. Letting these wounds breathe, giving them a voice, is the beginning of a transformative journey.

Allow yourself the grace of vulnerability. In a world that often equates vulnerability with weakness, dare to challenge that notion. For vulnerability is not a chink in your armor; it's a testament to your courage. It's an affirmation that you're brave enough to face your true self, to embrace it, and to grow from it.

As you journey inward, let the essence of self-love guide you. It's not about the cosmetic enhancements, the transient joys of material possessions, or the fleeting praises. True self-love is about acknowledging every facet of your being, however luminous or dark it may be, and understanding that your worth isn't determined by societal metrics. Your worth is intrinsic, immutable, and infinite. So, embark on this journey with an open heart and an open mind, and discover the universe that lies within.

Life isn't a Movie, and That's Okay

Real talk - we aren't all sunshine and rainbows. Movies, series, the media, all feed us a binary - good versus evil. The pressure to always be the 'good' guy is not only unrealistic but also suffocating.

It's why villains often resonate with us more. Their imperfections remind us of our own, and that's strangely comforting.

Let me bare it all. Yes, I aim for kindness. But hey, I'm not Mother Teresa. Sometimes I'm selfish, sometimes I screw up. So what? The journey is about embracing these imperfections, not burying them.

Self-love isn't about bubble baths and spa days (though those are nice). It's about digging deep, understanding your patterns, acknowledging your shadows, and just being unapologetically YOU.

Remember, you're not defined by society's skewed standards. You're unique, with your quirks and flaws, and that's what makes you, YOU.

So, are you ready for this journey of self-discovery? Let's dive in. After all, the real treasure is uncovering the gems within you.

II. The No-Bullshit Link Between Knowing Yourself and Loving Yourself

"To know thyself is the beginning of wisdom."-Socrates

Let me be brutally honest with you: you're a mess. No, I'm not throwing shade, and this isn't a peppy self-help mantra either. It's just the candid, naked truth. Each one of us is a beautifully complicated amalgamation of thoughts, desires, dreams, fears, regrets, and god knows what else. Trying to make sense of that whirlwind within? Good luck, buddy.

Remember when you bought that DIY furniture piece and you had this delusion that you'd ace the assembly? But then two hours later, you're sprawled on the floor amidst an array of oddly shaped pieces, contemplating if you'd ever see a fully formed coffee table. Welcome to the DIY project of understanding oneself.

Just when you think you've got a handle on who you are, your mind pulls a sneaky on you. Suddenly you hate strawberries, that band you adored is meh, and why the hell did you think green was your color? Our minds are ever-evolving, constantly shifting paradigms, and that's what makes this journey so darn intriguing.

The Uncharted Territory of Your Mind

"The mind is its own place, and in itself can make a heaven of hell, a hell of heaven." - John Milton

I've spent countless hours in my own head, navigating its winding lanes, revisiting memories (not always the fun ones), and confronting my inner demons. During the lock-in phase of the pandemic, oh boy, my mind was like a chatty neighbor on steroids, incessantly jabbering. But instead of playing the mute game or drowning its noise with yet another binge-watching session, I decided to engage.

Remember that night when you drunk-texted your ex or made a complete fool of yourself at a party? Yep, those cringe moments are up there, rent-free, playing on loop. But instead of squirming away, I sat with those memories, dissected them, understood them. It's kind of like popping that zit; it hurts initially but feels satisfying afterwards.

Mind Dates

No, not the dates you swipe right for. These are intimate, deep, introspective dates with your thoughts. And the best part? No reservation required, just a willingness to face yourself. These dates involve confronting everything - the good, the bad, and the downright embarrassing.

And here's what I discovered: facing your fears, regrets, and traumas isn't about self-flagellation. It's about understanding, forgiving, and, ultimately, freeing yourself. It's kind of like mental decluttering. Imagine Marie Kondo-ing your thoughts, holding each one, and asking, "Does this bring me joy?"

Don't just exist, live

Often, in the midst of all the chaos, we forget to truly live. You're not just a robot programmed to work, eat, sleep, and repeat. You're a beautiful, chaotic whirlwind of emotions, memories, dreams, and desires. So, cherish every laugh, every tear, every little quirk that makes you, well, YOU.

The Verdict?

Your journey to understanding yourself isn't going to be a breezy road trip. There will be detours, roadblocks, and yes, some soul-crushing traffic jams. But it's worth it. So, embark on this self-expedition with gusto, patience, and a good dose of self-love. After all, as Oscar Wilde beautifully quipped, "To love oneself is the beginning of a lifelong romance."

Figuring Out the Mess That is You

*"The Only Person You
Should Try to Be Better
Than, Is the Person You
Were Yesterday."
-Unknown*

So, picture this: I'm sitting in this run-down classroom with stained windows, and Mr. Henderson, this balding guy with glasses too big for his face, throws out a challenge. He says, "Bet none of you could talk about yourself for as many minutes as your age without stuttering or pausing." We all roll our eyes, but here's the kicker, he adds, "And I don't mean the bullcrap titles you show off on Instagram. I mean the raw, unfiltered you."

At that moment, I thought he'd lost a few screws. I mean, wasn't that what yearbooks and graduation speeches were for? But dude, he was on to something.

You see, we've all got these badges we wear. Some like medals, others like scars. Successful. Lonely. Rich. In love. Loser. Adventurer. Introvert. The kind of shit that society slaps on us or we eagerly put on ourselves. But strip away those labels, and what's left?

Remember being a toddler? No? Well, think of the last baby you cooed over. They didn't give a crap if you were the CEO or if you just got ghosted. They just saw... you. The baby didn't ponder over whether you're wearing Gucci or thrift-store specials. They just giggled if you made a goofy face. Their genuine laughter? Man, that's more valuable than any applause at a board meeting.

Why? 'Cause there's purity in that. An innocence we all had, but lost somewhere between kindergarten and our first job interview.

But where did we go wrong? When did we trade our authenticity for Instagram likes and Facebook relationship statuses? Who decided that our worth is determined by tags?

See, the world's got this giant bloody label-maker, and it's eager to stamp one on your forehead. 'Ugly', 'Too emotional', 'Not leadership material', 'Always the bridesmaid'. But here's the kicker: We let it. I did, too. I was labeled 'Not Beautiful Enough' at a freakin' funeral, for god's sake! But the nastiest labels? They're the ones we stick on ourselves.

Labels can chain you. Remember when you were called the "Class Clown"? Suddenly, you felt you always had to be funny. Got termed "The Responsible One"? Now, you can't even take a break without guilt. We become slaves to these labels, and even worse, we slap them on others, unknowingly or knowingly chaining them too.

Take a step back. Do you really want to reduce your entire complex, beautiful existence to a single, shitty label? 'Cause I don't.

I'm not just "that guy who writes stuff." I'm the guy who loses himself in the beauty of a sunrise, can down five cups of coffee and still sleep like a baby, and occasionally sings off-key in the shower. We're these intricate tapestries woven from experiences, dreams, fears, love stories, and heartbreaks.

Don't let one thread define the whole damn masterpiece.

Start by ripping off those suffocating labels. Let others see the swirling mess and magic that's the real you. And every time you're about to slap a label on someone else, hesitate. Think of the baby. Would the baby label them? No? Then neither should you.

At the end of the day, life's too short to play by someone else's rulebook. The journey to self-discovery isn't a one-time trek up the mountain. It's a daily adventure. A wild, unpredictable roller coaster that you've got a front-row seat to.

And here's the cheat code: You can't be pigeonholed if you keep evolving. Let 'em try to figure you out. Keep them on their toes.

Become a mystery, an enigma, a constantly shifting maze. And maybe, just maybe, in that chaotic dance, you'll stumble upon the pure, unlabelled joy we once knew as kids. So, here's to rediscovering and embracing the unlabelled, kickass version of you. Cheers!

Ditching the Bullshit: Finding Yourself by Nixing What You're Not

Alright, let me break this down for you with a little tale from my own roller coaster of self-awareness. When I first dipped my toes into this treacherous ocean of self-exploration, it felt like diving headfirst into a whirlpool. It was a shitstorm. No user manual, no map. Just me trying to make sense of the chaos inside.

Picture this: Young Dave, eager to figure himself out, scribbling down in his journal, trying one self-help book after another, all while making countless mistakes along the way. A hot mess? You bet. But in this chaos, a golden nugget of advice shone through:

"Dude, if you can't pin down who the hell you are, at least figure out who you definitely aren't."

Yeah, it sounds counterintuitive, but stick with me here. It's often simpler to pick out what repels you than what draws you in. Remember that high school party where everyone was doing that *thing* you just didn't jive with? Maybe it was chugging beer like water, and you were more of a soda kinda person. That's a clue right there.

Your Mission, Should You Choose to Accept It:

Grab a journal, your phone, a napkin - whatever's handy. Each day, set aside just 5 minutes (yeah, that's shorter than your coffee break). Note down something that doesn't resonate with you and the 'why' behind it. The magic? It's like creating a filter for the nonsense. You'll start recognizing what truly matters to you, cutting through the noise and refining your authentic self.

Now, here's the kicker, and listen closely: Hold those cards close to your chest. Yeah, I know, in a world where everyone's broadcasting their lunch on social media, this seems backward. But not every schmuck out there can handle a different perspective. Ever wonder why so many folks just nod along with the majority? Fear. They're terrified of being the black sheep, afraid of confrontation.

Do yourself a favor: Save your thoughts for the right audience. I've had my fair share of awkward dinners because I blurted out an unpopular opinion. And trust me, it's not worth the indigestion. Not everyone's ready for your brand of truth. Sometimes, just listening can teach you a thing or two. Doesn't mean you have to buy into it, but understanding where someone's coming from? Priceless.

Here's a snippet from my past: College Dave, surrounded by party animals. Booze flowing everywhere, but not once did it touch my lips, even with friends practically shoving it in my face. Was I being a prude? Nah. It just wasn't my scene. I wanted buddies who got that, who vibed with my kind of crazy.

The real power move? Once you've slashed through the BS and know what you're NOT about, you start attracting the right tribe. It's like they say,

---

"Your vibe attracts your tribe."

The garbage? It takes care of itself. There's a reason I don't have 5000 friends on Facebook. Quality over quantity, always.

Stand your ground. Not in a "holier-than-thou" way, but in a "this is me, take it or leave it" way. When you truly know what you're NOT, it's a heck of a lot easier to see what you ARE. And that, my friend, is where the magic happens.

Chapter 4 - Why Solitude is the Ultimate Self-Love

"You cannot be lonely if you like the person you're alone with." - Wayne W. Dyer

---

Remember when you were a kid and you'd throw tantrums just to get an extra cookie? Now you're reading a self-help book, hoping for a sprinkle of wisdom to convince you that spending time alone isn't equivalent to having spinach stuck in your teeth. But here's the tea: I'm not your fairy godmother, and I won't sprinkle magical words to make you feel better.

Why? Because seeking external validation is the first sign that we're missing the whole damn point. We crave constant hand-holding and a GPS voice saying, "Turn left here, champ!" But when that voice goes silent, we freak out and think we've ended up on the lonely road to Nowhereville.

You see, everyone has their own GPS set to different destinations, and as much as you'd like to think otherwise, not everyone is headed where you are. Along the way, people will take exits, stop at diners, or even have a flat tire. You can either pull over and lament the departures, or you can keep cruising.

Ever met someone who dances gracefully on life's tightrope, even when there's no safety net beneath? That's Maya for you. Allow me to share her story, one that's not just about finding oneself, but also about the strength that radiates from inner solitude.

Maya's life often reminded me of a beautiful but challenging ballet performance. As I saw her transition through the stages of life, there was a recurring pattern. Just when she got the steps right, the music would change. From shifting schools to navigating the complexities of friendships, her journey had its share of stumbles.

During high school, there was Sophie, her confidant, her duo in the dance of life. Yet, when life's choreography changed, their paths diverged. College seemed like a fresh start, and along came Zoe, the perfect partner for the next act. But as unpredictable as life can be, a sudden interlude separated their duet.

However, Maya's narrative was destined for a plot twist. Post-Zoe, she found her troupe, a group of girls whose spirits resonated like harmonious chords. They danced together, sharing stages, steps, and stories. But the finale of college signaled the end of this ensemble. As the curtain fell, their group numbers turned into solo performances.

Now, you might think this is just another tale of fleeting friendships. But no, this is about Maya and how she gracefully pirouetted through every twist and turn. Romanticized TV series and films had painted this rosy picture of ever-lasting friendships. Remember *Gilmore Girls*? Constant coffee dates and endless conversations. Reality, though, had a different choreography.

Here's the revelation: 'Forever' doesn't mean a perpetual duet. It's the occasional group dance, the sporadic duo, and the frequent solos. Maya taught me that. She embraced her solos, mastering every step, every move, with grace and passion.

In the end, it's not about finding the perfect dance troupe, but learning the choreography of one's own heart. Maya is a living testament to this. Her dance, her journey, remains an inspiration. It's a reminder that in the theater of life, solos can be as powerful, if not more, than group performances.

In retrospect; Here's a sobering truth bomb: Forever doesn't mean holding hands and skipping into the sunset. In today's age, 'forever' is reduced to a comment on an Instagram post or a fleeting memory of better times. And that's okay. The narrative that someone will always be there for you, rain or shine, is as real as unicorns. People aren't accessories you can wear or discard based on your mood. They have their lives, battles, and aspirations.

The key isn't to chain someone to your side. It's to be content in your own company. Find solace in your solitude. Befriend the person staring back at you in the mirror. When you enjoy your own company, every interaction becomes a delightful bonus, not a crutch you lean on.

To wrap this up, I'm not urging you to become a hermit. No! Cherish the gems in your life. But remember to also value your own presence. Being alone can be a party where the guest of honor is YOU.

Ready to turn this party into a full-blown carnival? In the next section, we'll delve into harnessing solitude for personal growth. Embrace your solitude, see it as a gift, and let's take strides towards your dreams. Game on?

Part Two: Mastering the Fine Art of Enjoying Your Damn Self

Chapter 5 - The Hardcore Guide to Embracing Solitude Without Going Insane

"To be alone is to be different and to be different is to be alone."
- Sylvia Plath

Let me tell you about Cassius Malloy. No, not the textbook stuff you can google in three seconds, but the human side. Born in the urban sprawls of Detroit in 1992, Cassius was a testament to the struggles of the modern age. The digital age was on the horizon, and Cassius was at the heart of it. Born to a family of tech geeks, he was gifted a computer before he could even utter his first word. While most kids were playing catch, he was 'coding'.

By the age of 10, he had developed small gaming apps, gaining small-scale recognition in the tech community. But like all true artists, Cassius wasn't content. He felt something was amiss. Studying in Silicon Valley, Cassius was surrounded by the latest tech, the fervor of startup culture, and an environment that was perpetually 'online'.

However, a chance seminar by a tech-detox advocate changed Cassius's direction. Much like how Dow had changed O'Keeffe's perspective on art, this seminar was Cassius's epiphany. He realized that amidst all the screen lights, he was losing touch with the light within.

One evening, Cassius stumbled upon an article about Bhutan — a country that measured success not by Gross Domestic Product but Gross National Happiness. It piqued his curiosity. On an impulse, he packed a bag, left his Macbook behind, and boarded a plane to Bhutan.

In the quiet valleys of Bhutan, Cassius rediscovered himself. No Wi-Fi, no gadgets, just him, the mountains, and his thoughts. Here, he didn't code for apps but scribbled in journals, introspecting. Cassius found his rhythm in the melodies of Bhutanese folk songs and the tranquility of the monasteries. This was his New Mexico, his sanctuary.

This transformative journey didn't turn Cassius against technology. Instead, he returned with a vision: to create tech that enhanced human connection, not replaced it. Using his insights from Bhutan, Cassius developed apps focused on mental well-being, digital detoxes, and promoting real-world interactions.

This urge to find solitude isn't unique to Cassius. Ever heard of Vincent van Gogh? The guy basically turned his solitude and "emo" feels into stunning art. Instead of complaining about loneliness, he painted Starry Night. Instead of joining the trending 'Feeling Lonely' hashtag on Twitter, he said, "Though I am often in the depths of misery, there is still calmness, pure harmony, and music inside me."

Today, we've got our noses buried in our phones, desperately swiping for human connection, thinking solitude is a bad Wi-Fi signal. Companies are profiting from our fear of missing out and our need to feel constantly connected. But the thing is, solitude isn't about disconnecting from the world; it's about connecting with oneself.

Look around. Those grinding day in and out, burning the midnight oil, or just diving deep into their passion? They're not the ones documenting every moment on Instagram. They cherish their solitude because it lets them focus. Like Malloy, they know that to create, to truly find oneself, sometimes you need to drown out the noise.

In the end, solitude isn't about being alone; it's about being with yourself. And trust me, that's one relationship worth investing in.

"In a World of Distractions, Laser-Like Focus is Your Freakin' Superpower."

You ever notice how everyone's hooked to their screens like they're IV drips of digital dopamine? Yeah, I've been there, scrolling like a madman at 2 a.m., thinking I'm feeding my brain, only to realize it's the same ol' junk food for thought. Let's not kid ourselves: our devices own us. Yes, even you, Greg, in the back, claiming you're "multitasking". Spoiler alert: you're not.

Ask yourself: How many times have you Googled, 'how to not get distracted?' or watched YouTube videos about 'maximizing productivity'? It's like asking a thief for advice on home security. Absurd, right?

So, what's the real deal? Why, when we swear off Facebook, do we find ourselves deep-diving into cat videos an hour later? Because, amigo, our minds have been hijacked. These tech overlords have turned our brains into notification-craving zombies. And trust me, there's no tutorial or 5-step plan that's going to un-zombify you.

Do you need someone else to tell you how to focus? That's like needing instructions to breathe. C'mon, mate. We don't need to 'learn' how to focus, we just need to remember how. And to do that, you've got to reclaim your mental real estate.

Now, let's talk solitude. Remember Cassius Malloy? He didn't need no app to remind her to take a break from the world. She chose isolation because she knew that in silence, the world's chatter fades, and your true voice emerges. If you constantly surround yourself with other people's opinions, your own voice gets drowned out. And seriously, if you're just an echo chamber for the five dudes you hang out with most, how will you ever discover your own badass tune?

But, let's be real. Not everyone can just pack up and find their own Bhutan like Mallory did. Yet, everyone can carve out a bit of solitude. Maybe it's just turning off your phone for an hour, taking a walk without earbuds, or sitting in a room doing absolutely nothing.

Your best ideas, your boldest thoughts, your most profound epiphanies – they don't come when you're knee-deep in notifications.

They come when you're truly alone, with your own untamed thoughts. So, if you want to tap into your purest form of genius, learn to embrace solitude. Not as an escape, but as a path to meet the most intriguing person you'll ever know: You.

"Mental Junk Food: Why Your Brain's Not Built for Binge-Watching."

Ever binged on pizza to the point where moving feels like you've been asked to scale Mount Everest? And breathing? A whole Olympic sport? Yep, I've been there, one regretful slice away from becoming the pizza itself. Then I wonder why I can't sprint a marathon immediately after.

Think of our minds like our stomachs. Stuff it with junk, and you're going to feel like crap. Eat the right stuff, in the right amount, and you'll function like a well-oiled machine. Would you eat burgers for every meal and expect abs of steel? Hell no. So why, in the name of all things sacred, do we bombard our brains with constant digital crap and expect it to perform like Einstein?

You wouldn't force-feed your gut non-stop for hours, right? We all know the drill — munch, feel full, take a break, repeat. Yet, with our brains, it's a non-stop Netflix binge of information, opinions, and god-knows-what. We're expecting our brains to churn out innovative ideas when they're practically drowning in random trivia about how many times a hummingbird flaps its wings or which Kardashian did what.

Here's a newsflash: Just like those greasy fries won't get you a six-pack, endlessly consuming internet drivel isn't going to sculpt a genius brain. Our minds, much like our bodies, have a simple motto: Garbage in, garbage out.

But the real zinger? While you're gobbling up the latest influencer's "top 10 ways to live your best life," you're not giving your brain a chance to, well, *think*. Let's get real: influencers, YouTubers, authors, they're just humans like you and me. They aren't some divine beings bestowing eternal wisdom. Their advice isn't one-size-fits-all. So before letting their thoughts set up camp in your mind, how about scrutinizing them a bit?

Inside each of us is an inner universe, a fountain of original thoughts, ideas, and reflections. But if we're always plugged in, always 'on,' we're never truly connecting with ourselves. It's like we've become DJs, constantly remixing other people's tracks and never creating our own music.

Now, I get it. Sitting alone, letting your brain wander? It's challenging, especially when there's an ocean of memes and TikToks waiting to be explored. We've conditioned our minds to thrive on this cheap, fast-food entertainment. So when it's time to buckle down, read, study, or work? Our brains are huffing and puffing, struggling to focus. Why? Because we've turned them into lazy couch potatoes.

Our daily mantra?

"Train the brain to resist
the mundane."

Yeah, digest that.

Getting some solitude might be tough. It's like going to the mental gym after ages. But trust me, your brain's begging for a breather. Take time to digest and reflect. Sift through the information overload, cling onto what's meaningful, and toss out the trash. That silence? It's the sound of your brain detoxing, regaining its mojo, and prepping for the next round.

In essence, give your mind its much-needed 'me time.' It'll thank you, not with abs, but with clarity, creativity, and a renewed zest. So, kick back, unplug, and remember:

*"Daily Brain Detox:
Because Mental Flab is
a Real Drag."*

The Beauty of Being Blissfully Bored

Ever been stuck at a family gathering where Uncle Joe rambles on about his glory days, and you're fighting the urge to pull out your phone and drown in Instagram stories? Yeah, that's boredom for you. But here's the weird thing: those moments of utter boredom? They might just be the golden ticket to your most genius ideas.

Back when I was a wet-behind-the-ears writer, starry-eyed and naive, I'd fawn over interviews of big shot authors. Almost every single one of them threw out this weird tidbit: their best ideas didn't pop up while in some intense brainstorming session, but rather during those moments when they were doing... absolutely jack shit. It sounded like an artsy thing to say until it happened to me.

Look, our lives are basically one long blur of emails, Netflix binges, Instagram scrolling, and, oh yeah, more emails. In this never-ending stream of content and distraction, where the hell is the pause button? Without that break, we end up becoming poor imitations of our Netflix watch history and Twitter feed.

I started testing out this "do nothing" theory by spending more time with, well, me. With every moment of just letting my mind wander, some of the most vibrant, original ideas began to sprout. It's like giving your brain the equivalent of a spa day — letting it chill without dumping more information into it. And voila! Fresh, groundbreaking thoughts emerge from seemingly nowhere.

Here's the truth bomb: a mind that's always running on fifth gear will, at some point, crash and burn. Just like you can't guzzle down five espressos in a row without turning into a jittery mess, you can't overload your brain and expect it to churn out Picassos and Hemingways.

Have you heard of the Italian concept from Elizabeth Gilbert's 'Eat, Pray, Love'?

Dolce Far Niente: the deliciousness of doing squat. Yep, it's about diving headfirst into the pure joy of doing sweet nothing.

In our "always-on" world, we're so damn afraid of missing out or not being productive every waking second. But here's the twist: mastering boredom is a radical act. It's choosing to be okay with stillness, with quiet, with the absence of 'doing.'

The way I see it, getting good at being bored is a high-level meditation skill. You're there, with all the craziness inside your head. The first few times? It's gonna suck. Your brain will pitch a fit, dredging up that embarrassing memory from high school or making you second-guess that text you sent. But stick with it.

With every boredom session, you're giving your mind the canvas to paint new ideas. You're learning to steer it gently when it starts to spiral. Over time, not only does this make you a creative powerhouse, but you also get to Jedi-master your brain, reigning in impulsive desires and learning to stay as serene as a monk on vacation.

So, challenge yourself to embrace the void. Cultivate the fine art of being blissfully bored. Your brain, creativity, and sanity will thank you. And who knows? Your next masterpiece might just be a boredom session away.

Mastering the Art of Self-Sufficiency

"In a world obsessed with connections, the truest one is the connection with yourself."

Alright, let's get something straight: life's a fickle friend. Today's "forever" promises might become tomorrow's ghosting texts. Sounds grim? Welcome to the real world, baby.

Look, we're living in a time where chasing your dream might mean leaving your hometown barbeques and Sunday brunches with friends. You might pack your bags for that fancy job in a new city, or for some academia rush in a college miles away. Shit happens. People change. Your favorite Netflix shows even get canceled. And in this whirlwind, if you haven't mastered the art of being your own anchor, you'll feel like a ship lost at sea every time life tosses a storm your way.

Sure, wrap yourself in the warm blanket of love, be it family, friends, or that special someone. Relish those moments. Laugh loudly. Cry together. Share that damn dessert. But at the same time, be the badass who can also Netflix and chill...alone.

A pal of mine, let's call her Sarah, dated her boyfriend for a whopping 5 years. She built her world around him so much that when he moved cities, she felt like her life's GPS was kaput. She rang me up, voice shaking, saying, "My entire world orbited around him. Now, it's like I'm floating in space with no planet to call home."

I dished out advice then that I'll lay out for you now: Think of your life as a vibrant mosaic. People, passions, hobbies—they're all individual tiles that make up the masterpiece. So, yeah, it's okay if one tile goes missing or changes color. The mosaic is still beautiful, still complete. Love your squad. Dive into that weird stamp-collecting hobby. Maybe even talk to your plants (hey, no judgment). Point is, create a life so radiant and rich that love oozes out of every nook and cranny, in all its forms.

The golden rule? Always belong to yourself first. That way, your bonds with others are built not out of desperate necessity, but out of genuine mutual respect and affection. Being with others becomes a choice, not a survival strategy.

Now, if you're nodding along and thinking, "Hell yeah, I want to be that rock-solid, self-sufficient ninja!" then let's dive deep. Let's transform those solo hours into soulful, growth-packed adventures. Game on?

Chapter 6 - Loneliness: Not a Curse, But a Fucking Growth Spurt

"Embrace yourself fully, for even if you resist, you remain the same. Revel in your essence." -
Inspired by Garden Spells

Embracing the Art of Solitude:

"You Alone, Complete."

Picture this: I've wrapped up college and am right back in my tiny hometown. The kind of place where everyone knows what you had for breakfast and how you like your coffee. I was lost. Lost in the vast emptiness of not knowing my purpose, my drive. No fancy job title, no groundbreaking business idea. Just me, my thoughts, and societal pressures playing peek-a-boo from every corner. Shit was tough.

Ever been in a dark room, searching for a light switch, only to realize you're holding the flashlight the whole time? That was me. I was searching for external solutions to an internal void. The one person who was MIA from my life's ensemble was, well, me.

But here's the kicker. We all play this game. We champion the shit out of our friends' dreams, pushing them toward greatness. Hell, we've got our own stock of pep talks and motivational monologues that could give Tony Robbins a run for his money. But the minute it's our turn, we toss that golden playbook out the window and snuggle up with self-doubt.

Why are we epic wingmen for others but total cockblocks for ourselves? Why is it so damn hard for us to be our own cheerleader? Isn't it crazy that no class in school ever taught us the art of befriending ourselves?

So, here's the game plan: Let's flip the script. Time to be your own hype squad. Let's transform those lonely moments into phases of explosive personal growth. Ready to roll?

Chapter 7 - Meet Your New Buddy: It's You (Surprise, Bitch!)

"Life isn't about finding yourself. Life is about creating yourself." - George Bernard Shaw

Let me drop a little 30-something wisdom on you. When I was in my 20s, there was this societal script I was "supposed" to follow: party hard, chase fleeting romances, vibe to songs whose lyrics escaped me, and dub it all as "living life." But here's the thing, none of that was my jam.

Instead, I was this oddball with dreams of success juxtaposed with a yearning for a serene life in a quaint Scottish village. A cocktail of ambition and tranquility. Confusing? Maybe. Amazing? Hell, yes.

I realized early on that the route to my dreams wouldn't be lined with frequent pub nights and casual hangouts. Friends are great, but their dreams might not align with yours. So, faced with a choice between following the herd or carving my path, I picked the solitude of ambition. It was a no-brainer really, especially since moving back to my hometown kind of narrowed down my social circus.

Fast forward to now, I've got this ever-present buddy who's been my anchor. This pal pushes me, challenges me, and gives me that cocky grin whenever I feel like I'm on top of the world. Now, I'm betting you want an introduction.

Meet your goals. Yep, that's my evergreen friend. Goals are the catalysts that transform mundane days into tales of conquest. So why not redefine your loneliness? Convert it into a productive, goal-crushing powerhouse session. That empty silence? Think of it as the applause waiting to happen once you nail that objective.

I get it. This might sound like a motivational TED Talk on steroids, but remember the old Shaw wisdom I started with? It's all about creation. And to create, my friend, you need to harness that solitude.

Now, you might be bobbing your head, thinking, "Sounds rad, but how?" Well, the journey from solitude to success starts with a single step: befriending your ambition. Once you're ready to embrace that, flip to the next page, and let's chart out the route to becoming BFFs with success.

Chapter 8 - Drafting Your 'Life Doesn't Suck' Blueprint

"Success usually comes to those who are too busy to be looking for it." - Henry David Thoreau

So, you want to slap a "been there, done that" sticker on the universe, huh? Welcome to the club. We've got jackets. But here's the rub: if I ambushed you with a mic and a spotlight and asked you to define your version of success, what would you say?

Most would jump to, "I want a house so big it needs its own zip code, money like Scrooge McDuck, and an Instagram-worthy life where I brunch in Paris and dine in Tokyo." Now, if everyone's painting the same bloody picture of success, doesn't that seem a tad... unoriginal?

Look, it's not a crime to desire money. Hell, in my 30s, I had a borderline inappropriate love affair with it. But the circus of modern success? It's making us all perform like clowns. We're sold this idea that success is about that designer bag, a romantic proposal beneath a world-famous tower, or raising a prodigious toddler who can quote Shakespeare and solve calculus problems.

The issue? We're chasing a carbon-copied dream, worried that if we stray, we'll be labeled weird or out of touch. We're so desperate to fit into the cookie-cutter mold of success that we've forgotten to ask: what the hell do I actually want?

We're in this bizarro game where we're racing to keep up, not with the Joneses, but with every Tom, Dick, and Harry flaunting their "perfect" lives on Instagram.

Your dream isn't a designer brand, it's supposed to be uniquely yours.

If money's your game, cool. But define it. If you're aiming for $10,000 a month, then what's your game plan for the first hundred? You're not Harry Potter; you can't just wave a wand and expect gold coins to pour from the sky.

Or maybe you're on a spiritual quest, looking for some Zen in the chaotic circus. Great, but how? Occasional meditation sessions where you mentally scold yourself for not achieving Nirvana don't count. Regular practices? Those matter. Wanting peace isn't enough; you've got to work for it.

At the end of the day, it's your dream. Define it. Chase it. Just make sure it's really yours and not something borrowed from someone else's highlight reel.

"Being yourself is the hardest thing in the world to do, but it's also

the most worthwhile." -
Mark Manson

Okay, real talk. This isn't me trying to kick you while you're down. But let's face it: if your roadmap to success is sketchier than a toddler's doodle, you're basically screwed. You can't chant "I want to be successful" in front of a mirror and expect shit to materialize.

Being on your lonesome might sound like a punishment in today's hyper-connected world, but it's actually your ticket out of this mess. Solitude? It's not the monster under the bed; it's the therapist on your couch. When you're solo, the cacophony of the world dims, and you're left with the one voice that matters: yours. All those times you've been steamrolled by the crowd? You probably didn't know where you stood because you never stood alone.

I've been in that maze. Hell, there was a time when if I had to choose between pizza or pasta, I'd need a UN summit. Asking everyone and their dog for advice was my jam. I couldn't decide if I wanted a latte or cappuccino without conducting a survey. But solitude changed the game for me. It was like my psyche finally got a clear line and my desires, authentic and unfiltered, began to transmit.

This herd mentality? It's like the Wi-Fi of modern life – everywhere. We cling to the majority because standing out feels like standing on a landmine. Venturing alone seems daunting because, well, it's bloody unfamiliar.

But come on, aren't you sick of this rat race? Tired of chasing a mirage of beauty defined by, I don't know, Kardashian standards? Worn out from trying to climb a ladder without knowing what's at the top? And the real kicker: aren't you petrified of ending up like a knockoff version of everyone else, never truly embracing your essence?

Here's your takeaway, a nugget if you will:

"Craft your narrative, your definitions. Don't slap a generic label on your life because it's trending."

'To Thine Own Self Be True" - William Shakespeare

"NOT EVERYTHING THAT GLITTERS IS GOLD, BUT SOMETIMES, IT'S THE CHEAP GLITTER THAT EXCITES US THE MOST."

Listen up, and this is important: We've been handed one of the most complex, marvelous pieces of machinery in existence – the human brain. And yet, most of us treat it like an old storage unit, stuffed with societal norms, expectations, and half-remembered song lyrics. And then, at the end of the day, we scratch our heads and wonder, "Why does happiness feel like a missing sock?"

Time to flip the switch, not on your dusty old lamp but on that beautiful gray matter upstairs.

How? It's like customizing your own life's menu instead of ordering the same overpriced, mediocre combo meal everyone's munching on. Why be content with a generic coffee mug when your life is waiting for its own unique design?

I tossed out a thought on Insta about squeezing joy from the mundane. Someone shot back, "I still don't get how to find my joy." Ouch. We're so engrossed in swiping right on other people's lives that we've swiped left on our own essence. If you're here hoping I've got a three-step recipe to your personal joy or success, might as well use this page as kindling. Your story isn't mine. Your pulse accelerates for reasons uniquely yours.

It's like expecting a universal shoe size to fit everyone. Sure, it might fit some, but for others? Blisters city.

What's happiness to you? Maybe it's the whiff of fresh pastries or dancing in your PJs at 3 AM. Success? Is it a corner office view or a hammock in your backyard? Sketch out your own blueprint. You can't erect your life on someone else's foundation.

Command your narrative. Let's move past being societal puppets with someone else pulling the strings. Even if you don't wear a crown, act like your life's the kingdom and you're the monarch. Your brain? It's not just for storing memes and dad jokes. Dive inward, and you'll find it's also a compass.

It's high time you started painting with your own palette. Let's do this!

Chapter 9 - No More Talk: Your Kick-Ass Solitude Action Plan

"The unexamined life is not worth living." -
Socrates

"Growth isn't always about adding; sometimes, it's about figuring out what you've got too much of."

Ever stared at a cluttered garage and thought, "Damn, where do I even begin?" That's life for many of us. Overflowing with past regrets, bad habits, and Netflix binges. Everyone says they want a "glow up," but if you don't know which part of you needs some re-polishing, how're you going to shine?

Why change? Pop quiz: name two reasons. Not for me. For yourself. If you're scratching your head harder than you do on a tricky crossword, then you're just in for another pumped-up pep talk that'll dissolve faster than sugar in hot tea.

Let me give you an analogy. You've got this wild, overgrown garden - that's your life right now. The 'dream life' you're chasing? That's the same garden, but manicured, blossoming, maybe even with a cheeky gnome or two. Spotting the difference between the two? That's your job. But don't just stop at what flowers you want; think about the soil, the weather, even how the damn sun shines.

Think of it like this: Your "dream life" isn't some distant mountain peak. It's how you lace up your boots and walk every damn day. It's that simple.

Got it? No? Here, let me paint it clearer: *Life doesn't just one day sprout fairy wings and sprinkle you with pixie dust. You tweak it daily, stitch by stitch.*

So, as cliché as it sounds, grab a piece of paper. No, seriously. Now, jot down 5 things that irk you about your current life.

Maybe it's that soul-sucking job. Or perhaps it's that new fad diet you tried that made you fart unicorns. Ain't nobody going to list out your peeves for you. Get to it before you're in your twilight years, cursing every missed opportunity.

If you don't dissect who you are right now, how're you gonna craft that badass future self? Sometimes, it's not all sunshine and self-love. Occasionally, you gotta put on those critical glasses and squint hard at the mirror. It's not about beating yourself up; it's about acknowledging that you, like everyone, have areas to grow.

There's this dangerous brand of self-love that's like, "I'm perfect; I fart rainbows." No, champ. There's a fine line between self-love and delusion. Embrace who you are, but also fist bump the amazing person you're becoming. And trust me, a dash of honesty now saves a ton of regret later. So, quit the fairytales, face the music, and get to rewriting your story.

Facing the Mirror: The Raw Truth

"Self-deception is the stingiest trickster; it can hustle you out of your dreams faster than you can blink."

Let's get real here. Before you demand the world to hand you authenticity on a silver platter, how about handing a bit to yourself first? There's a particular brand of irony in chasing after authenticity when you're a maestro in playing pretend with your own damn self.

Sure, there's a circus of people out there, dazzling you with mismatched words and actions. Welcome to life's three-ring shitshow. You'll bump into folks that'll say they've got your back, but when push comes to shove, they're nowhere in sight. While their questionable song and dance are out of your hands, how brutally real you get with yourself is very much in your court.

Deep down, there's this inner compass in you. An innate BS detector. You know when you're being treated as an afterthought rather than a priority. You sense when you should be hitting the exit rather than sticking around for another round of disappointment. But hell, our brains are slicker than a car salesman on commission. They whisper sweet little lies, telling you to delay that gym session, scarf down those late-night tacos, or gift that flaky friend one more chance.

True, self-honesty is like swallowing a bitter pill. It's facing those ghoulish fears head-on, with no place to hide. But here's the kicker: once you get raw with yourself, a surreal kind of clarity kicks in. It's like cleaning muck off a window and finally seeing the view. You'll feel a surge of satisfaction, knowing that you're acting in your own best interest.

So, stop outsourcing your truth. Start by facing that person in the mirror, and demand more. Because the cornerstone of real satisfaction? It begins with raw, unfiltered self-honesty.

Step 1: The Single Pebble Ripple Effect

"The man who moves a mountain begins by carrying away small stones." – **Confucius**

Alright, let's cut the crap. Have you ever tossed a pebble into a pond and watched the ripples spread? Now, imagine throwing a boulder instead. You'd get one big splash, and then... it's gone. That's basically how most of us approach change. We muster up the strength for one big splash, and then we're out of breath, drenched, and standing there thinking, "What the hell just happened?"

Many of us, in a caffeine-fueled frenzy of ambition, decide we're gonna change EVERYTHING—right now, this second! We sign up for a marathon (despite hating jogging), swear off sugar (though our love for donuts is eternal), and decide to meditate every morning at 5 am (even if the last time we saw 5 am was during a Netflix binge).

I remember back in 2015, when I decided I was going to be a 'New Dave.' I had this mental checklist: killer abs by February, write a bestselling book by May, and, oh yeah, find inner peace somewhere in between. But by March, the only six-pack I had was in the fridge, and the closest thing to inner peace was deciding which Netflix show to watch next.

Here's the unfiltered truth: aiming for everything is the quickest route to achieving nada.

Now, let's circle back to the pebble. Focusing on one thing is like that single pebble causing ripples across the entire pond. Mastering one aspect of life doesn't just give you that warm fuzzy feeling of achievement; it also sets off a chain reaction of other positive changes.

My buddy, Jeff, wanted to kick his soda addiction. That was his pebble. Just one can of cola, he decided to quit. Not the pizzas, not the late-night chips binge, just the soda. Six months in, not only did he ditch the carbonated devil, but he found himself making healthier choices overall, without it feeling like a Herculean task. Today, Jeff's ripple effect means he's 20 pounds lighter, and he can climb three flights of stairs without sounding like a wheezing accordion.

So, challenge time: Ditch the boulder. Pick up that metaphorical pebble. What's one small thing you can change? That one thing that's been nagging at you, no matter how trivial it seems. Because once you set that ripple in motion, you'll be amazed at how far it goes.

Pause. Reflect. Identify. Because our next step? We're going to dive deep into transforming that singular piece of your puzzle into a masterpiece.

Step 2: The "Do One Damn Thing" Method

"You don't have to be great to start, but you have to start to be great." – Zig Ziglar

Ever heard of the **K.I.S.S. principle? Keep It Simple, Stupid**. Yeah, it sounds a bit sassy, but let's face it, we often need a little sass to get off our asses and into gear.

Now, don't get me wrong, motivation is a beautiful, fleeting beast. We've all been there, right? You watch that one awe-inspiring TED Talk and you're ready to change the world. But by Thursday, you're back to debating whether pizza is a complete meal (it's not, but damn it's good) and if binge-watching romantic comedies counts as cardio.

Flashback to my disastrous attempt to become "Healthy Mark." My vision was grand: I'd do yoga at dawn, have green juices for breakfast, and by dinnertime, I'd practically levitate with wellness. Predictably, by day three, my 'green juice' was a Margarita, and yoga was just a fancy word for stretching to grab the TV remote.

But remember the pebble? Here's the sequel: The "Do One Damn Thing" method.

Instead of setting these grandiose, vague "I'm gonna change the world" plans, I picked just one tangible action. One. When I embarked on This Book writing journey, I zeroed in on this singular action: Write one page, every single day. No if's, and's, or but's. And guess what? It worked.

So what's an "Action Goal?" Well, in Manson lingo, it's doing one damn thing that clearly sets you on the path you want to tread. No fluff, no maybes. You pick an action and you stick to it, come hell or high water.

For instance, my buddy, Dan, wanted to lose weight. Instead of joining the hottest new fitness cult or going keto-crazy, he just decided to walk 10,000 steps daily. Sounds too simple, right? Fast-forward six months, and he's dropped 20 pounds and added a whole bunch of healthier habits, all spurred by that one daily commitment.

So here's your mission, if you choose to accept it (and you better): Grab a post-it note, slap it somewhere you can't ignore, and write down one clear action related to your BIG ISSUE. This is your non-negotiable, daily task. And then? Just do the damn thing. Every. Single. Day.

Step 3: The "You Do You" Philosophy

"Don't watch the clock; do what it does. Keep going." – Sam Levenson

Now, if there's one thing to know about humans, it's this: we're a tad bit complicated. We have this nasty habit of shoving square pegs into round holes. And, when they don't fit? We beat ourselves up.

Case in point: I was once on this quixotic mission to be a member of the 5 AM Club. You've probably heard about the myriad benefits of waking up at the crack of dawn. Hell, I even dove headfirst into books like Robin Sharma's 'The 5 AM Club' and 'The Miracle Morning'. Compelling reads, both of them. To top it off, I religiously watched countless YouTube videos on morning routines. But, here's the kicker: I. Just. Couldn't. Wake. Up.

No matter how much I tried, I'd fail miserably, and my mom fondly started referring to me as "sleeping beauty". Cute, right? But why was waking up early such a Herculean task for me? Turns out, it wasn't laziness. I stumbled upon the idea of circadian rhythms and the fact that not everyone's wired to be an early bird. Some folks, like me, are night owls, and they thrive post-sunset.

This realization was more than liberating. It was a lesson in understanding my own rhythms, my personal "groove," if you will. If I'm in my element writing and creating at midnight, then why the hell was I forcing myself to be a morning lark?

Now, here's the crux: everyone's on this self-improvement train, setting goals left and right. Yet, most jump ship midway. Why? Because adopting someone else's "best practice" can sometimes feel like wearing a straitjacket. It's restrictive, uncomfortable, and just not you.

Case in point, my 2023 goal: scribbling down one pages daily for this book. Traditional wisdom might suggest I tackle this first thing in the AM. But I'm not about that life. Writing isn't a chore for me; it's a passionate dance. So, I do it when the mood strikes, whether that's at 2 PM or 2 AM.

Similarly, when it came to fitness, I didn't want the routine grind of a gym. Some days, I bust out some killer dance moves in my living room, and on others, I feel the wind on my face as I cycle. It's all about feeling alive and doing things my way.

Catching my drift here? It's crucial to tailor your path towards goals based on your unique mojo. It's not about forcing a square peg into a round hole; it's about finding the perfect fit for that peg. And remember, you're ever-evolving; what feels right today might not tomorrow. So, stay fluid, stay adaptable.

In summary? Get to know yourself, cherish your quirks, and embrace the "You

Do You" philosophy. Now go forth, shake things up, and get started on your epic journey. TODAY.

Chapter 10 - Getting High on Your Own Supply: Making Alone Time Your New Drug

"We accept the love we think we deserve." - Stephen Chbosky

Okay, let's get real here for a sec. You ever wonder why some folks light up your day like a damn Christmas tree, while others feel like a perpetual Monday morning? It's simple. With the right crowd, time feels like a Ferrari on the Autobahn. It's fast, exhilarating, and you just can't get enough of it. They're the human equivalent of your favorite playlist—full of love, inside jokes, those awkward hugs, and sometimes, the soul-baring kind of conversations.

But then, there are those other folks. The ones who feel like a slow-motion replay of the most boring game ever. With them, every second feels like a painfully stretched-out eternity. They're like that annoying song you just can't get out of your head— repetitive, grating, and leaving you wondering, "Why the hell did I even listen to this?"

But, here's the kicker, and brace yourself for this truth bomb: sometimes, *you* can be that annoying song to *yourself*. If you're still scratching your head, let me spell it out: your relationship with yourself might be in the "I'd rather be anywhere but here" category. No joy, no love, just pure, unadulterated "meh."

Case in point: I moved back to my old stomping grounds and my so-called "buddies" ghosted me. Fast forward to now, they're blowing up my phone, wanting to hang. But guess what? The thrill's gone. Old me would've been down in a heartbeat, but current me? I've got shit to do, shows to binge, and frankly, I'd rather hang with my own damn self. Why? Because I've turned my own company from drab to fab.

So, what's the takeaway? Learn to enjoy your own vibe. Make your alone time so bloody fantastic that you're not desperately seeking validation elsewhere. It's a game-changer. And how you do that? Well, pull up a chair. Let's dive in.

1. Find Your Own Damn Joy

"It's not how much we have, but how much we enjoy that makes happiness." - **Charles Spurgeon**

Let's get one thing straight: life isn't here to spoon-feed you joy. Ever wonder why as kids, everything was an adventure, but as adults, even binging a series feels like a chore? Childhood was all about chasing fireflies, exploring new games, and just pure, raw, unfiltered joy. Flash forward a few decades, and we're here, looking for the next dopamine hit from a like on our Instagram post.

You see, adulthood came with responsibilities and a crap-ton of expectations, snuffing out those embers of happiness. We became the expectation-driven, treadmill-running, sad-sack adults waiting for the world to throw us a joy-bone. Ask yourself this: When was the last time you did something purely for kicks? Not for productivity, not for someone else's validation, but for your damn self? If you're taking more than three seconds to answer, you're doing it wrong.

I've been there. Looking around and thinking, "Is this it?" Hell, at one point, my hometown felt like a dull void. No parks (and I'm a nature junkie), no libraries (total bookworm here), and not a single art gallery in sight. But whining about it? That's the easy route. Instead, I decided to mine my environment for bits of happiness. Those evening walks? They became my window to the world. Instead of cityscapes, I had narrow alleys, old houses whispering tales of days gone by, and fleeting moments with strangers that tickled my storyteller spirit. For me, it was the difference between existing and living.

Here's the deal: Joy isn't a distant cousin you'll bump into at a family reunion once in a while. It's that needy pet demanding your attention, and it's on you to carve out those moments. Could be in the warmth of your morning coffee, the comfort of a favorite song, or hell, even cooking with candles and some Frank Sinatra in the background.

Seek out those slivers of joy intentionally, deliberately. Why "intentionally"? Because it's damn easy to slip into the abyss of blame and bitterness. When you take charge, finding joy becomes a delightful treasure hunt. Whether it's the aroma of fresh rain or the mischievous grin of a toddler, magic is everywhere. Your task? Hunt it down.

Either you chase joy, or you let the grind chase you. The ball's in your court.

2. Quit the BS and Get Learning

Ever had that wild itch? Not the one that requires a medical ointment, but that burning urge to pick up something new, something exciting. Yet, you brush it off with the classic, "I'll do it someday." I've been there. Hell, we all have. I've dreamt of being that guy in the pool doing fancy strokes, the dude artfully jotting down calligraphy notes, or throwing in a casual "Guten Tag!" at parties. But what stopped me? Time? Nah. Reality check: It was plain, old, unsexy laziness masked with excuses.

We're knee-deep in the information age, people. Everything — from knitting tutorials to learning Swahili — is just a click away. And yet, here we are, hours deep in the black hole of TikTok, instead of, say, practicing the salsa moves we always dreamed of. Classic!

It took me a while, but the epiphany did strike. Time wasn't the real villain here. My award-winning self-deception skills were. Look, I recently dove headfirst into crocheting. Yeah, you read that right. Crocheting! My nights transformed from mindless binge-watching to visualizing patterns, textures, and crafty stuff. The satisfaction? Unparalleled. Each stitch, each loop brought a sense of achievement, a zest for life beyond the humdrum of daily routine.

I'm not asking you to pull out needles and yarn. Heck, that might not be your jam. But there's something out there that gets your pulse racing, whether it's shredding on a guitar, mastering a perfect risotto, or, hell, juggling. The joy isn't in becoming an expert overnight but in those tiny victories, those baby steps.

So here's the challenge: Scrap the excuses. Set aside that 15 minutes a day. Dive into whatever the hell floats your boat. Let it be the spark, the thing that sets your soul on fire.

It's not about filling time but about enriching it. It's about growing, evolving, and owning your alone time. So, next time solitude beckons, make sure it's not just you lounging in PJs. It's you, levelling up, one hobby at a time.

3. Brain Gains: Trading Fiction for Frickin' Wisdom

Alright, gather around, party animals. Let's talk about a lie that's been sold to us more times than those fancy green juices that promise to detoxify your soul. We're fed this notion that reading is lame and bookworms are the geeks of the nerd universe. Hollywood and pop culture have done a stellar job painting the wild 20s as a decade of booze, parties, and occasional lapses in judgment.

Knowledge-seekers? Pshh, they're the ones living in their moms' basements, right? And the cherry on this crap-cake? Our education system. It's like a one-size-fits-all hat that's *definitely* not fitting all. We're force-fed information, assessed on subjects we didn't even choose, and then branded based on scores. Can't blame you for running away from books post that trauma. Hell, I'd run too.

But here's the twist: it's not the books; it's the way they were shoved down our throats.

Enter my life circa 2020. Yours truly, in the middle of a breakdown, quarantine doing no favors. But then, Robin Sharma's 'The Monk Who Sold His Ferrari' lands on my lap. I devoured that book like it was the last piece of pizza at a party. And boom, just like that, I was hooked. Went from "ugh, books" to "more books, please!" in a span of weeks.

Since then, books became my dope. They transformed my perspective, schooled me on life, mistakes, wins, everything. They filled voids professors left, became companions, and played the role of the wise old sage. You know how they say words have power? I'm living proof.

Books, done right, aren't these dusty old things on a shelf. They're life's cheat codes. They're ticket stubs to a million different worlds. They're mentors, therapists, and best friends rolled into one. But, and it's a big

BUT, you've got to break that mold society set for you. You've got to find what lights your fire.

Expand that horizon beyond books too. Podcasts, TED Talks, online classes – the buffet is endless. Be ravenous for knowledge. Heck, drown in it. Your brain is not a trash can, so why feed it garbage?

So next time you're chilling solo, don't just Netflix and nap. Read a chapter. Listen to that talk. Hell, find out why the sky is blue if that's what gets you going. Remember, every day's a school day if you want it to be. The universe is one big lesson, waiting for you to tune in. Don't just pass through life, crush it with the power of words.

Exercise: Your DIY Brain Buffet: Serving Fresh Knowledge Daily

"The mind once enlightened cannot again become dark."- **Thomas Paine**

You remember those old-school scrapbooks? The ones where you'd paste random memories and feel all artsy about it? Yeah, let's do a 21st-century version of that, but this time, it's for your brain.

Step 1: Whether you're tech-savvy or old-school paper-lover, grab a device or a notebook. Heck, grab a chisel and a stone tablet if that's your thing.

Step 2: Label that beauty, "FOOD FOR THE SOUL." If that's too vanilla for you, throw in some exclamation marks or emojis. Go wild.

Now, this isn't just another folder or notebook. Oh no. This is your personal mind gym, where every tidbit of information you gobble up is a weight lifted. This is your one-stop-shop for every nugget of wisdom you gain.

Dived into a **TED Talk during lunch?** Jot down the gems you picked up. Read an intriguing book about space sloths (or something more grounded)? Fill in the cool stuff. Got a mentor or someone who's just bloody brilliant? Dedicate a page to them – a mini shrine of inspiration, if you will.

This notebook/folder/tablet (you rock-age dwellers) is more than just pages or files. It's a symbol, a neon-lit sign that screams, "Hell yeah, I'm growing!" It's your badge of honor that you're not letting life just swish past, but rather, wringing out every last drop of wisdom from it.

Bottom line? Time's ticking. And while some may be content watching it go by, you've got the tools to seize it, mold it, and make it dance to your tunes. Educate, elevate, and for heaven's sake, enjoy the ride. Because, in the grand game of life, it's always better when you're having fun leveling up.

Chapter 11 - The Ultimate Freedom: Becoming Your Own Damn Hero

"DANCE LIKE NO ONE'S WATCHING, BECAUSE, WELL, NO ONE IS"

"To be yourself in a world that is constantly trying to make you something else is the greatest accomplishment." -
Ralph Waldo Emerson

There's a silly image I've carried with me since college. It's of me, a legend in my own mind, in the heart of this awesome party or traversing some kickass city with a group of friends who are as wild and free-spirited as I imagined myself to be. But here's the twist: in reality, most of my college days were spent doing...well, not that. Instead, I was the dude staring at his shoes too shy to mutter a 'hey.'

My life's been a series of epic trailers with somewhat less epic main features. College? Thought I'd be Indiana Jones, but was more of a Bilbo Baggins pre-adventure. Traveling the country post-college? Envisioned myself as a modern-day Marco Polo, but barely made it past two cities.

But here's a truth bomb: often, our grand expectations of fun revolve around other people. It's like we're constantly scripting these perfect ensembles cast movies in our heads. But reality ain't Hollywood, and sometimes, your co-stars don't know their lines, forget their roles, or don't even show up for the shoot.

Now, does that mean you just sit around, cursing the universe for not making your life a Spielberg film? Hell no.

There's a little life hack I stumbled upon, which I think is the grown-up version of "if you want something done right, do it yourself." Ready for it? **"Do the things you wanted to do with others, but rock them solo."**

Want to go to that rave? Who needs an entourage? Groove to your heart's content. Dreaming of that Mediterranean cruise? Embark on a solo voyage, and who knows, maybe you'll become the captain of your own ship (metaphorically, of course). Yearning for a movie night? Your couch, your popcorn, your rules.

By focusing on being your own best company, you're not only staying true to yourself but also ensuring that your happiness isn't outsourced. Because, at the end of the day, the best dance parties are sometimes the ones you have in your living room, in your pajamas, with no one watching.

> *"The greatest thing in the world is to know how to belong to oneself." - **Michel de Montaigne**

Remember those cheesy scenes from teen movies where everyone has this rad sleepover? Lit candles, bowls of junk food, and the latest heartthrob flashing across a screen? I'll be honest, I was that guy who secretly wished he could be a part of that scene, just with less hormonal drama and more R-rated humor.

Post-college, the dream of that "perfect" sleepover felt as real as me getting abs after one gym session (Spoiler: it never happened). We all got buried under the so-called 'grown-up' stuff. But here's a revelation I had on a particularly lonely Friday night: Who says you can't have your own damn sleepover?

So, I did. Lights dimmed, candle scent wafting through the room, my favorite pasta dish by my side (because, priorities), and a Christmas movie. Hell, in December, I even threw in "Die Hard" for good measure. It's a Christmas movie, fight me. It felt like I stepped out of the relentless rat race and into a bubble of nostalgia and comfort.

See, the thing was, I didn't need a posse to validate my quirky movie nights. I took the reins of my own imagination and said, "Screw it. I'm the director of this show."

Then there's the picnic saga. 40 minutes out of town, I've got this grassy haven. Just me, my Kindle, some scribbles in my journal, a bit of crochet action, iced coffee (because apparently, I have an addiction), and the world's best doughnut. Okay, maybe not the best, but it's up there. It's the kind of "me-time" that rejuvenates the soul.

If I had a parental bone in my body, I'd be that annoying dad pushing you out the door, yelling, "Go find your picnic spot!" or "Host your solo movie marathon!"

You've been sitting on the bench waiting for others to pass you the ball of fun. Screw that. You're the MVP of your own game. Plan a date night with numero uno: you. Selfies in cool places? Do it. Redecorating? Why not. The love letter you wish you got from that crush in 11th grade? Write it to yourself, because you're fabulous.

Buy yourself that plant — not just because they're trendy, but as a green reminder that you're growing and thriving on your own terms. And when you hit those big life milestones, don't shy away from patting yourself on the back, shouting from the rooftop, "Damn, I'm proud of me."

After all, if you're not your biggest fan, who will be?

"Dear Me: The Brutally Honest Love Letter You Never Knew You Needed"

*"The most powerful relationship you will ever have is the relationship with yourself." - **Steve Maraboli***

Alright, let's cut the crap for a second. I want you to think about the last time you genuinely hung out with the most crucial person in your life: You. Not sure? That's what I thought. It's time for a wake-up call, and it starts with a pen and paper.

The whole "write a letter to yourself" thing might sound like a rejected therapy exercise, but bear with me. What if you wrote an "I've been a shitty friend to myself" letter? That's right, call yourself out on your own BS. When was the last time you treated yourself? When did you last acknowledge your achievements, no matter how small?

Jot down every single time you side-stepped your dreams because it wasn't "the right time." Remember that dress or shirt you saved for a "special occasion"? Hell, every day you're alive is a special occasion.

Want to buy yourself flowers or a damn good cup of coffee? Go for it. But do it like you mean it. And if you're planning a date night with numero uno, don't half-ass it. Dress like you're meeting the love of your life, because guess what? You are.

Start seeing the actions you take for yourself not as an afterthought, but as a grand romantic gesture. Crank up the intensity, add a bit of flair, and be bold in your pursuits.

Bottom line? Stop sidelining yourself. Dive headfirst into making every gesture, every self-love act, a blockbuster event. Because in the grand movie of life, you're the main act, the director, and the damn critic.

Give yourself a performance worth raving about.

Here's a tough pill to swallow: Life's like a massive potluck, and you've got to bring your own damn dish. Expecting others to spoon-feed you your dreams? Well, prepare for a long wait and an empty plate.

You see, everybody at this proverbial dinner party called life is elbow-deep in their own plates, hunting for their version of the gourmet experience. If you're standing at the side, waiting for someone to pass the mashed potatoes or pour the wine, you're going to be left with crumbs.

So, what's the play? Grab a plate. Better yet, be the one who brings the most exciting dish to the table. Explore the vast menu life offers. Sample the spicy, the sweet, the savory. Heck, throw in a bit of bitter for the full experience.

This book? Think of it as your culinary map. A nudge to remind you of all the flavors waiting out there. Because, let's face it, nobody's coming with a silver platter. You've got to roll up your sleeves, dig in, and savor every bite on your own terms. Why? Because at the end of the day, you're your own chef in this grand feast. Make sure your plate is damn unforgettable.